AF422945

Shattered Praise

Shattered Praise

12 Devotions for When Worship Feels Hard

PASTOR JOHN DAVID SMITH

Scribe & Canvas Publishing

South Carolina

Hardcover ISBN 979-8-950061-00-4
Library of Congress Control Number: 2026941468

Published by **Scribe & Canvas Publishing**™
Pendleton, SC | www.scribeandcanvas.com

Interior and cover design by **Elev8d Designs**
Printed in the United States of America

10 9 8 7 6 5 4 3 2 1

To the weary worshipers—
the ones who show up with trembling hands, cracked
voices,
and broken hearts.

To those who have loved and lost, hoped and been hurt,
believed and still broken.
This book is for you.

For the hallelujahs whispered through tears.
For the faith that keeps flickering, even in the dark.
May you know that your offering is seen,
your story is sacred,
and your worship is enough.

THE AUTHOR'S VOICE

*These devotions are written not only
from the desk but from the shepherd's walk.*

Dear Reader,

There's a certain kind of worship that doesn't get sung on Sunday mornings.

It doesn't come from mountaintop moments or miracles answered in real time.

It comes from hospital rooms.

Empty chairs.

Late-night cries that echo into silence.

It comes from disappointment, loss, fatigue—and still believing.

This is where *Shattered Praise, Unbroken Faith* was born.

I'm not writing from the other side of the pain with every answer tied up in a bow.

I'm writing from the midst of it—where faith sometimes shakes,

where praise feels like a whisper,

and where God proves Himself faithful in the quiet, again and again.

If you're in that place, too—this book is for you.

I pray you find yourself on these pages,

and more importantly, I pray you find God there, too.

— *Pastor John David Smith*

INTRODUCTION:

For Every Broken Hallelujah

There are seasons when faith feels effortless—when songs come easy and hope is loud.

But there are other seasons, too.

Seasons when grief steals your voice.

When prayers feel like echoes.

When worship is not a declaration, but a decision.

This devotional was born in those seasons.

Inspired by the song *Broken Hallelujah* by Mandisa, this book is a journey into the heart of honest praise—not the kind that rises when everything makes sense, but the kind that rises when nothing does.

Here, you'll find devotions for the weary, the questioning, the barely-holding-on. You'll find stories, Scriptures, breath prayers, and space to reflect.

But most of all, I pray you find room to be honest—with God, with yourself, and with your worship.

You don't need to wait until you're healed to offer praise.

You don't have to be whole to be heard.

Bring what you have.

Even if it's broken.

Especially if it's broken.

Because God meets us there.

And He calls even that—especially that—holy.

TABLE OF CONTENTS

* * *

DEVOTION ONE:
The Power of a Broken Hallelujah

Scripture Anchor:

"The sacrifices of God are a broken spirit;
a broken and contrite heart, O God, you will not despise.
— Psalm 51:17

Opening Reflection

There are seasons when songs don't rise—they stall.

They sit heavy in the chest, caught somewhere between breath and breaking.

Grief tightens the throat.

Disappointment floods the soul.

And the melody you once carried with ease now feels distant—like it belonged to someone you used to be.

In these moments, worship can feel out of reach.

Like something reserved for stronger days.

Clearer days.

Days when you felt whole.

But worship was never meant to belong only to the healed.

Some of the truest songs are not sung from stages—but from valleys.

Not with strength—but with shaking.

Not with clarity—but with clinging.

We've been taught to associate praise with victory.

With answers.

With joy that makes sense.

But there is another kind of song—quieter, deeper, costly.

A song in ruins.

A broken hallelujah.

It doesn't rise because life is good.

It rises because God is still good.

It doesn't shout—it sighs.

It doesn't rush—it stays.

It doesn't resolve—it reaches.

And heaven does not reject that sound.

It leans in.

Because praise that costs you something carries a weight comfort never could.

So if your worship today is fragile… fractured… unfinished—

bring it anyway.

God has never required perfection.

Only presence.

And even now—especially now—

your broken hallelujah is still holy.

Devotional Insight

In Mandisa's song "Broken Hallelujah," we are reminded that God never asks for perfection. He asks for presence. Not for polished verses, but honest ones. When life falls apart, praise becomes a courageous act. We worship not because we feel whole, but because we trust the One who holds our brokenness.

Sarah didn't plan to worship.

She was just trying to survive the night.

The house was too quiet.

The bed too wide.

The silence too loud to ignore.

Grief had taken her language.

Even prayer felt like too much effort.

But somewhere between exhaustion and surrender... she started humming.

No lyrics. No strength. Just breath finding sound.

And then—one word:

"Hallelujah."

It wasn't strong.

It wasn't steady.

It barely made it past her lips.

But heaven heard it.

Because God has never measured worship by volume—only by honesty.

Scripture is full of worship offered through tears. David wrote laments that became sacred hymns. Job, in his grief, said, "The Lord gave and the Lord has taken away; blessed be the name of the Lord." Worship in pain is not a contradiction—it is a declaration that God is still worthy.

A hallelujah that survives pain is a hallelujah that has learned truth.

Your broken hallelujah is not second-rate. It is not lesser than joyful praise. In fact, it might be the most truthful offering you ever give. And God receives it with delight.

Guided Questions for Reflection

1. When have I offered God a song from a place of sorrow or emptiness?

2. What prevents me from believing that broken praise is still beautiful to God?

3. How might I create space in my life for worship that is raw, honest, and unfiltered?

Breath Prayer / Affirmation

God, I offer You what I have. Even in pieces, it is still praise.

Closing Prayer

Lord, I come with what I have—a heart that is aching, a voice that trembles, and faith that sometimes feels fragile. Take my broken hallelujah. You are worthy even when I don't understand. Even when joy is absent and songs falter, You are present. Thank You for receiving the offerings I bring, however shattered they may seem. Amen.

Your Reflections

Write what is real—your thoughts, your questions, your prayer.
Let honesty be your offering.

(Space to Breathe)

(Space to Breathe)

* * *

DEVOTION TWO
Trusting God with a Broken Heart

Scripture Anchor:

"Trust in the Lord with all your heart and lean not on your own understanding; in all your ways submit to him, and he will make your paths straight." — Proverbs 3:5-6

Opening Reflection

Faith feels natural when life makes sense.

When prayers are answered quickly.

When the road is clear.

When your heart is still intact.

But when everything breaks—

faith changes.

It loses its ease.

It sheds its certainty.

It stops feeling like confidence and starts feeling like resistance.

Not a declaration—but a decision.

Not a song—but a struggle.

Not clarity—but surrender.

Because when your heart is broken, trust is no longer automatic.

It becomes intentional.

It becomes costly.

It becomes a choice you make in the dark.

Trusting God in pain is not about pretending everything is okay.

It's about refusing to believe that everything falling apart means God has.

It's choosing to hold on—

When nothing feels stable.

When nothing feels certain.

When nothing feels fair.

It's lifting your eyes when everything in you wants to close them.

It's whispering, "Even now… even here… I still believe."

And that kind of faith—

the kind that trembles but doesn't let go—

is not weak.

It is sacred defiance.

Devotional Insight

Scripture does not give us polished faith—it gives us persistent faith.

Job lost everything—his children, his health, his stability. His friends misunderstood him, his prayers met silence. And yet, in the ashes, he said, *"Though He slay me,* *yet will I hope in Him."* That wasn't blind optimism. It was defiant faith.

Hannah prayed through grief and humiliation. Misjudged and overlooked, she still returned to God, believing her sorrow was heard.

Jesus, in Gethsemane, fell to the ground in anguish. He knew what was coming and still surrendered: *"Not My will, but Yours be done."*

These acts of trust were costly. Because real trust—especially in pain—always is. And maybe you've been there too. When the loss came. When the call shattered everything.
When God felt silent.

You didn't have answers.

But something in you whispered, *"Hold on."* That whisper is faith.

Faith isn't the absence of struggle. It's the decision to keep reaching—even with trembling hands. It's crying on the bathroom floor and still believing He's near. It's waking up to a day you didn't want and hoping anyway.

That kind of faith is sacred. God doesn't overlook it. He honors it. He meets you in it.

That whisper—"hold on"—is not small.

It is not fragile.
It is not insignificant.
It is faith in its purest form.
Not loud enough to impress people.
But strong enough to reach God.

Faith is not proven by how you feel—it is revealed by what you hold onto.

Guided Questions for Reflection

1. What does trusting God look like for me right now?

2. Where do I struggle to believe He is working in my pain?

3. What would it mean to surrender, even without full understanding?

Breath Prayer / Affirmation

God, I trust You even when I cannot trace You.

Closing Prayer

Lord,
I bring You my broken heart.
I don't have all the answers.
I don't know how things will unfold.
But I choose to trust You.
Remind me that You are with me.
Strengthen my faith where it wavers, and draw me close when I feel lost.
I believe You are still writing my story.
Amen.

Your Reflections

Write what is real—your thoughts, your questions, your prayer.
Let honesty be your offering.

(Space to Breathe)

* * *

DEVOTION THREE
Finding Evidence of Grace

Scripture Anchor:

"Because of the Lord's great love we are not consumed, for his compassions never fail. They are new every morning; great is your faithfulness." — Lamentations 3:22-23

Opening Reflection

Storms come.

Sometimes they build slowly on the horizon, giving us time to brace ourselves.

Other times, they arrive without warning—crashing into our lives and leaving everything in disarray.

Either way, they leave a trail:
broken routines, broken hearts, broken expectations.

The loss of a job.

The unraveling of a marriage.

The diagnosis we didn't see coming.

The phone call that changed everything.

And in their wake, we begin to look for God.

We scan the sky for some sign that He is near.

But often, the thunder drowns His voice.

The rain blurs our vision.

And all we can do is hold on.

Faith doesn't promise to stop the storm.

It never has.

What it promises is presence.

That in the chaos, we are not alone.

That in the breaking, we are still being held.

God's faithfulness doesn't always arrive in grand gestures.

Sometimes it shows up quietly—

in the resilience to get out of bed,

in the unexpected phone call,

in the warmth of a shared meal,

in the strength to breathe again when you thought you couldn't.

God's compassions aren't a one-time gift.

They renew.

They return.

Not all at once—but exactly when we need them:

quiet, faithful, enough.

Enough to take the next step.

Enough to believe that even in the storm, grace still falls.

You may not be able to trace every moment of God's hand in this season.

But if you look closely, you may begin to see the evidence—

soft as mercy,

steady as sunrise.

God's faithfulness is not always loud—but it is always present.

Devotional Insight

David had just been turned down for another job.

The rejection email was short.

The bills were not.

His confidence had thinned to almost nothing.

As he left the store—head low, heart heavy—he stopped to help an elderly man load groceries into his trunk.

The man looked at him, smiled gently, and said, "Sometimes, the worst days are the days God is closest."

It was a simple sentence.

But it stayed with him.

It didn't change David's circumstances.

But it shifted something inside him.

That moment opened his eyes.

He began noticing things—not flashy miracles, but quiet mercies:

A friend who texted just when he felt forgotten.

A surprise refund check in the mail.

A moment of stillness where he could finally breathe.

God's faithfulness often arrives like that—

not in thunder or spotlight, but in fragments.

A whisper.

A kindness.

A breath you didn't know you had the strength to take.

Grace is not always dramatic—it is often daily.

And if you trace those moments—if you follow the thread—you start to realize:

grace was there all along.

Guided Questions for Reflection

1. Where have I seen God's faithfulness in a hard season?

2. What small signs of grace have I overlooked?

3. How can I begin a daily habit of remembering God's goodness?

Breath Prayer / Affirmation

God, Your grace finds me, even in the storm.

Closing Prayer

Lord,

Thank You for Your steady presence.

Open my eyes to the ways You are moving, even when I feel overwhelmed.

Remind me that You have never left me, and that Your faithfulness is written into every day.

Amen.

Your Reflections

*Write what is real—your thoughts, your questions, your prayer.
Let honesty be your offering.*

24

* * *

DEVOTION FOUR
Worshiping When We Feel Shattered

Scripture Anchor:

"The Lord is close to the brokenhearted and saves those who are crushed in spirit." — Psalm 34:18

Opening Reflection

What do you do when praise doesn't come easy?

When the music plays, but your heart is too heavy to lift a note.

When the words on the screen feel foreign.

When joy feels like a memory you can't quite reach.

Sometimes we think worship must be loud—overflowing with certainty, hands raised in triumph.

We imagine that to worship rightly, we must first be whole.

Put back together.

Strong and unshaken.

But what if that's not true?

What if the most powerful praise isn't the kind that rises from clarity, but the kind that rises from chaos?

What if God leans closer when our voices crack and our prayers falter?

Worshiping while shattered is not hypocrisy—it's honesty. It's bringing our fragmented selves before God and saying, *"This is all I have. But it's still Yours."*

It may be quiet. It may be tear-stained. It may not sound like much. But it is sacred.

Because worship is not about performance—it's about presence. And God draws near not to the polished, but to the brokenhearted. He sits with the crushed in spirit. He receives praise even when it comes in pieces.

So if all you can offer today is a whisper, a sigh, a silent tear—offer it.

God is not asking for perfect.

He is asking for *you*.

Devotional Insight

Emily didn't stop believing in God.
She just stopped feeling anything.
Depression settled like a fog.
Church became a place of pressure, not peace.
She couldn't sing.
Couldn't raise her hands.
Couldn't fake a smile.
So she stayed home—until one Sunday, something pulled her back.

She sat in the back row. The music played. People sang. She didn't. She just breathed. And in that moment, something shifted.

She wasn't performing or pretending. She was simply present. And that—though she didn't know it—was worship.

We often mistake worship for volume or expression. But sometimes, the most powerful praise is quiet.

It's sitting silently.

It's weeping in the shadows.

It's whispering God's name into the ache.

That, too, is worship.

Scripture doesn't say the Lord is close to the strong.

It says He is close to the brokenhearted.

He draws near, not to the polished, but to the shattered.

And in that nearness, worship is born.

So if all you have are fragments, bring them.

You don't need to be whole to be welcome.

You don't need to be loud to be heard.

You don't need to be healed to be held.

God is in the room.

Guided Questions for Reflection

1. What expectations have I placed on myself when it comes to worship?

2. How might God be inviting me to worship differently in this season?

3. What does "praise from the pieces" mean for me personally?

Breath Prayer / Affirmation

Even shattered, I can still worship.

Closing Prayer

God,

I bring You my praise, even when it's quiet.
Even when it feels incomplete.
You are worthy in every moment.

Thank You for meeting me in my brokenness and calling my worship beautiful.

In Jesus' name, Amen.

Your Reflections

Write what is real—your thoughts, your questions, your prayer.
Let honesty be your offering.

(Space to Breathe)

* * *

DEVOTION FIVE
Letting Go and Leaning In

Scripture Anchor:

"So do not fear, for I am with you; do not be dismayed, for I am your God. I will strengthen you and help you; I will uphold you with my righteous right hand." — Isaiah 41:10

Opening Reflection

Surrender is not weakness.
It's wisdom wrapped in humility.
It's not the waving of a white flag in defeat—it's the lifting of empty hands in trust.
Most of us are taught to hold on.
Hold on to our plans.
Hold on to control.
Hold on to how we thought life should go.
We grip tightly to what makes us feel safe—timelines, expectations, certainty. But life rarely honors those plans. And when it all starts slipping through our fingers, we scramble to hold on even tighter.

But there comes a moment in every journey of faith when God invites us to do the opposite.

To stop gripping and start releasing. To stop striving and start trusting. To surrender—not because we're giving up, but because we're giving over.

In broken seasons, surrender becomes sacred ground. It's the place where trust takes root and grows. Where we stop depending on ourselves and start leaning into the steady, unshakable hand of God.

Letting go doesn't mean you don't care. It means believing there's Someone bigger holding what you can't. It means trusting that even when it feels like everything is falling apart, God is still holding you together.

So breathe.

Loosen your grip.

And know this: surrender isn't the end of your strength—it's the beginning of His.

Devotional Insight

Mike was a planner. He mapped his life with precision—career, marriage, future—believing that if he did things the "right" way, life would follow suit.

But when his marriage ended, everything unraveled.

In the silence of his now-empty home, he faced a choice: hold tighter or begin to let go.

He chose surrender.

Not in one dramatic moment—but breath by breath, decision by decision.

He released his anger, his questions, his image of how life was supposed to be. And in that surrender, healing began.

Surrender isn't giving up—it's giving over.

It's opening your hands—not in defeat, but in trust.

It's saying, *"God, I don't understand, but I'm ready to be held."*

Letting go isn't passive. It's powerful.

It clears space for grace to move.

It makes room for peace to take root.

We resist surrender because control feels safe. But control is also exhausting. It weighs us down with burdens we were never meant to carry.

Surrender trades that weight for something better:

God's strength.

God's presence.

God's promise to uphold you with His righteous hand.

Surrender is where trust grows. Where healing begins. Where new stories are born.

So loosen your grip.

Lay it down.

And lean into the One who will never let you go.

Guided Questions for Reflection

1. What am I still trying to control?

2. Where is God inviting me to surrender?

3. What would it look like to lean into grace instead of resistance?

Breath Prayer / Affirmation

God, I release what I cannot carry. I trust You to hold me.

Closing Prayer

Lord,

I lay down my striving.

I let go of what I can't fix or figure out.

Help me to trust that You are working, even when I don't understand.

Teach me to surrender, not in defeat, but in devotion.

Amen.

Your Reflections

Write what is real—your thoughts, your questions, your prayer.
Let honesty be your offering.

40

* * *

DEVOTION SIX
Giving Thanks in All Circumstances

Scripture Anchor:

"Give thanks in all circumstances; for this is God's will for you in Christ Jesus." — 1 Thessalonians 5:18

Opening Reflection

Gratitude in hardship is not instinctive. It doesn't rise automatically when the world caves in or when our hearts are heavy with sorrow. In fact, thankfulness in the valley feels unnatural—like singing in a minor key when all you've known is harmony.

And yet, gratitude in the valley is one of the most profound acts of faith. It's choosing to notice the flicker of light even as the shadows stretch long. It's the quiet defiance of despair. It's a whisper that says, *"I may not see the whole picture, but I still trust the Painter."*

This kind of gratitude doesn't deny the pain. It doesn't sugarcoat loss or pretend that suffering is a gift. It simply refuses to let the valley define the whole landscape. It looks for God in the details—in the breath you didn't think you had strength to take, in the kindness of a friend, in the moment of peace that came unexpectedly.

It's giving thanks for the presence of God,
not just the absence of trouble.

Paul wrote his words about thankfulness not from a place of ease, but from experience with prisons, shipwrecks, betrayal, and loss. And still, he said: *"Give thanks in all circumstances."* Not *for* all circumstances—but *in* them. Because God's goodness isn't based on our surroundings. It's anchored in His unchanging character.

When you give thanks in the valley, you are planting seeds that will one day bloom in the light. You are declaring that darkness doesn't get the final word. And you are opening your heart to see the grace that has been there all along.

Gratitude in the valley is not easy.
But it is powerful.
And it will carry you.

Devotional Insight

Gratitude in hard places is not denial—it's discipline.
It's not pretending everything is fine. It's choosing to anchor your heart in something deeper than your pain.

Paul and **Silas** were beaten, bloodied, and imprisoned —yet at midnight, they sang. Not because life was good, but because God still was.

Their praise didn't change their chains right away.
It changed them.

David gave thanks while hiding in caves.

Habakkuk rejoiced even as famine swept the land.

Their gratitude wasn't circumstantial—
it was foundational.

You don't have to be thankful *for* the valley. You can be thankful *in* it. Because God hasn't left. Because grace still meets you. Because even here, beauty flickers through.

Gratitude won't always fix your situation. But it will soften your heart. Shift your lens. And open space for healing to begin.

When Mike began naming three small gratitudes a day, his life didn't change overnight—
but his vision did.

The job didn't come back. The relationship stayed broken. But he noticed more:

warm coffee,

a check-in from a friend,

a verse that lingered.

That's the quiet power of gratitude.

It doesn't erase pain. It reframes it. It doesn't shout. It steadies. It may not bring answers, but it keeps your heart open long enough for hope to find a way in.

So begin here. With one small thing. And then another. Let gratitude rise—not because life is easy, but because God is still good.

Guided Questions for Reflection

1. What small things can I thank God for today?

2. How has gratitude shifted my heart in past seasons?

3. What does it look like to practice thankfulness, even in pain?

Breath Prayer / Affirmation

Even here, I will give thanks.

Closing Prayer

God,

Thank You for being faithful in every season.

Open my eyes to see Your blessings, even in hard places.

Help me choose gratitude, not as denial, but as declaration.

You are good, and I trust You.

In Jesus' name, Amen.

*Write what is real—your thoughts, your questions, your prayer.
Let honesty be your offering.*

(Space to Breathe)

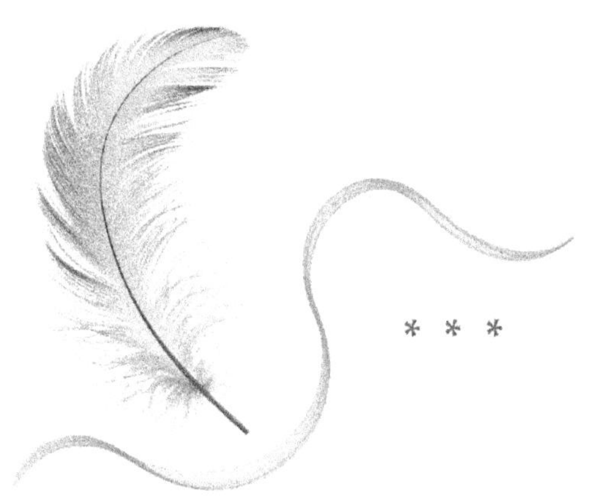

* * *

DEVOTION SEVEN

When God Rebuilds the Broken

Scripture Anchor:

"To bestow on them a crown of beauty instead of ashes, the oil of joy instead of mourning, and a garment of praise instead of a spirit of despair." — Isaiah 61:3

Opening Reflection

Redemption is not simply the undoing of pain. It's not a divine rewind that erases the suffering and restores life to what it once was.

Redemption is deeper.

Richer.

Holier.

Redemption is the transformation of pain into purpose. It's when God takes what should have destroyed us and uses it to develop us. It's when the very thing that broke us becomes the very place He begins to build something new.

God does not ignore our scars. He doesn't pretend the shattered places never existed. He rebuilds us *through* them—layer by layer, scar by scar. He shapes us not despite our suffering, but because of it.

We want beauty instead of ashes. God offers beauty *from* ashes.

We want joy in place of mourning. God brings joy *through* mourning. That's redemption.

In Isaiah 61, God makes a promise—not to remove all sorrow immediately, but to exchange it. He trades despair for praise. He covers shame with righteousness. He transforms the burned-out wreckage of what was into something astonishingly beautiful.

Your story is not beyond repair. Your heart is not too far gone.

Your ruins are not wasted in His hands. You may feel like you're starting over. But God never starts from scratch—He starts from scars. He rebuilds not on the absence of pain, but on the presence of His grace. And what He restores is always stronger, deeper, and more beautiful than what was before.

So bring Him the ashes. Let Him shape them into a crown.

Devotional Insight

The Bible overflows with redemption stories—not fairy tales, but true accounts of God restoring what seemed lost.

Peter denied Jesus three times, yet Jesus restored him—not with shame, but with purpose: *"Feed my sheep."* His failure became the foundation of his calling.

The Prodigal Son returned home in disgrace. But before he could explain, his father ran to him, wrapped him in love,

and celebrated his return.

The Woman at the Well carried years of rejection. After encountering Jesus, she ran back to her town—no longer hiding, but proclaiming: *"Come see a man who told me everything I ever did."*

These weren't perfect people. They were broken people made whole by grace. And God is still writing those stories.

You may feel like your past disqualifies you, that your pain has closed off possibility. But redemption doesn't begin when you have it all together. It begins when you bring Him what's left.

Your wounds don't cancel God's plan.

They often prepare you for it.

What once threatened to destroy you may become the very thing God uses to heal someone else. He doesn't erase the scars—He redeems them. He doesn't start from scratch—He starts from what's been shattered.

So bring Him your ashes. Your ruin. Your regret.

Let Him make beauty from it.

Let Him build something stronger than what was before.

Because in God's hands, broken doesn't mean finished. It means the rebuilding has already begun.

Guided Questions for Reflection

1.   What broken parts of my story have I seen God begin to restore?

2.   In what ways has pain shaped my compassion or calling?

3.   How can I share my story as a testimony to God's redeeming power?

Breath Prayer / Affirmation

God, thank You for rewriting my story with grace.

Closing Prayer

Lord,
  You are the God who restores and rebuilds.
  Take the shattered pieces of my life and craft something beautiful.
  Use even my deepest wounds to reflect Your love.
  Let my story become evidence of Your power to redeem.
  In Jesus' name, Amen.

Your Reflections

Write what is real—your thoughts, your questions, your prayer.
Let honesty be your offering.

(Space to Breathe)

* * *

DEVOTION EIGHT

Embracing Hope Beyond the Pain

Scripture Anchor:

"Offer your bodies as a living sacrifice, holy and pleasing
to God—this is your true and proper worship."
— Romans 12:1

Opening Reflection

Worship is more than music.
It's more than lyrics on a screen or melodies lifted on
Sunday mornings.

Worship is a posture—
a way of being, of breathing, of believing.

It is the quiet decision to live a life surrendered to God,
even when life doesn't look like we hoped it would.

True worship doesn't require everything to be perfect.
It doesn't demand certainty or clarity.
It simply invites honesty and presence.

Romans 12:1 urges us to offer our *bodies*—our whole
selves—as living sacrifices.

That means we bring to God not just our best moments,

but also our weariness, our wounds, our worries. It means showing up in faith even when we feel empty. It means trusting that our daily lives—yes, even the messy, unremarkable, broken parts—can be holy offerings.

When you choose to love in a season of heartbreak, that is worship. When you keep praying even when God feels silent, that is worship. When you care for others while your own soul aches, that is worship. When you open your hands and say, *"God, even now, I'm Yours,"* that is worship.

To live a life of worship is to become a living hymn— one that doesn't always rhyme or resolve, but still sings of hope. It's letting your life testify to God's goodness, even when your circumstances don't.

You don't have to be healed to worship. You just have to be willing. God receives your offering. And He calls it beautiful.

Devotional Insight

Worship isn't confined to church walls or Sunday mornings.

It's not limited to well-timed chords or powerful vocals. Worship is so much more than a song—it's a life lived in response to who God is, even when everything around us is falling apart.

Throughout Scripture, we see people worship not because life was easy, but precisely because it wasn't.

Mary, the mother of Jesus, praised God while carrying a promise she didn't yet understand. Pregnant, unmarried, and unsure of what lay ahead, she still declared, *"My soul magnifies the Lord."* She worshiped in the unknown.

David danced before the Lord, wild and unashamed, even though his journey had been marked by betrayal, heartbreak, and loss. He worshiped not from a throne of ease, but from a heart shaped by sorrow and intimacy with God.

Paul, imprisoned and beaten, lifted prayers and songs from behind bars. His surroundings didn't dictate his spirit. He praised not because he was delivered—but because he was devoted.

These weren't just acts of worship. They were declarations of hope. Each one of them made the bold decision to praise through pain—to trust in the middle of what didn't make sense. Their lives became offerings, their faith anthems rising from places of suffering.

Worship is not an escape from pain; it is an anchor within it. It tethers us to God when everything else feels like it's unraveling.

Every act of trust, every step of obedience, every whisper of gratitude—especially in seasons of grief or confusion—is worship.

It doesn't have to be loud to be real.
It doesn't have to be perfect to be powerful.
So let your life sing. Even softly. Even shakily.

Your quiet praise is not only heard in heaven—
it is cherished.

Because worship that rises through brokenness is worship that reaches the heart of God.

Guided Questions for Reflection

1. What does a life of worship look like for me?

2. How can I incorporate moments of worship into my daily routine?

3. In what ways has pain taught me to worship more deeply?

Breath Prayer / Affirmation

My life is worship. My pain still praises.

Closing Prayer

God,

Teach me to worship with my life.

Let my choices reflect trust in You.

Fill my ordinary days with sacred meaning, and let my pain be an offering that brings You glory.

In Jesus' name, Amen.

Your Reflections

Write what is real—your thoughts, your questions, your prayer.
Let honesty be your offering.

(Space to Breathe)

64

* * *

DEVOTION NINE
Finding Strength in Vulnerability

Scripture Anchor:

"My grace is sufficient for you, for my power is made perfect in weakness." — 2 Corinthians 12:9

Opening Reflection

In a world that rewards self-sufficiency, highlights achievement, and celebrates control,
admitting weakness can feel like failure.

From an early age, we're taught to be strong, to keep it together, to hide the parts of ourselves that don't measure up. We equate vulnerability with risk—and often with shame.

But the gospel tells a radically different story.

In the kingdom of God, weakness is not something to be covered up—it's something God leans into.
It is not a disqualification—it's an invitation.
Not a flaw—but a doorway.

Paul's words in 2 Corinthians 12:9 turn the world's

definition of strength on its head: *"My grace is sufficient for you, for my power is made perfect in weakness."*

God doesn't ask us to come to Him with polished strength.

He asks us to come as we are—with the fear, the fatigue, the flaws we've tried so hard to hide.

And when we do, He meets us there—not with judgment, but with grace.

It is in those moments—when we stop pretending, when we lay down our masks—that something sacred happens.

We stop striving and start receiving.

We stop clenching and start trusting.

And God, in His mercy, begins to show us that weakness is not the end of our story.

It's the beginning of His strength.

Devotional Insight

Paul, the tireless apostle and bold church planter, knew what it meant to wrestle with weakness.

He pleaded with God to remove his "thorn in the flesh"—a persistent source of pain or limitation.

And God didn't take it away.

Instead, He gave Paul something better: grace. And a promise. *"My power is made perfect in weakness."*

That wasn't just a comfort. It was a revelation.

Moses stammered through his self-doubt and begged God to send someone else. But God didn't look for a better speaker—He reminded Moses that His strength would speak through him.

Gideon was hiding in fear, convinced he was the least and the last—but God called him "mighty warrior," not because of who Gideon thought he was, but because of what God saw in him.

Jesus, in Gethsemane, wept and sweat blood in the most vulnerable moment of all—surrendering to the will of the Father with trembling words and complete obedience.

And through that vulnerability, salvation came to the world.

Weakness is not the enemy.

It is the entry point.

When you finally admit, *"I can't do this on my own,"* you are not disqualified—you are aligned with heaven.

That honesty is not a liability.
It's a lifeline.

It invites God to move—not just around your weakness, but *through* it.

So stop trying to measure up.

Stop striving to be "enough."

Let God's grace be sufficient.
Let His power rest on you—not in spite of your weakness, but because of it.

Guided Questions for Reflection

1. What area of weakness do I try to hide from others—or from God?

2. How might my vulnerability become a channel for God's strength?

3. What would it mean to boast in weakness, as Paul did?

Breath Prayer / Affirmation

In my weakness, God is strong.

Closing Prayer

Lord,

I am tired of pretending.
I am weary from trying to be enough.

I give You my weakness.
I ask for Your strength.

Let me see Your grace at work, even in what I'd rather hide.

In Jesus' name, Amen.

Your Reflections

Write what is real—your thoughts, your questions, your prayer.
Let honesty be your offering.

(Space to Breathe)

72

DEVOTION TEN
Worship Through Weeping

Scripture Anchor:

"You keep track of all my sorrows. You have collected all my tears in your bottle. You have recorded each one in your book." — Psalm 56:8 (NLT)

Opening Reflection

Tears have a way of making us feel exposed.

They come when our defenses break. When words fail. When the weight we've carried silently becomes too much to hold. And yet, in a world that often sees tears as weakness, God sees something altogether different.

God doesn't dismiss your tears.

He doesn't rush you past them.

He collects them.

Psalm 56:8 tells us that not a single tear we shed goes unnoticed. They are gathered by God—remembered, recorded, revered. In His kingdom, our tears are not signs of failure. They are signs of faith.

Because tears mean we've risked loving deeply.

They mean we still care.

They mean we've chosen to feel rather than go numb.

In the presence of God, tears are not interruptions to worship.

They *are* worship.

They are the liquid language of lament—raw, honest, and holy.

So don't hide your weeping. Don't rush to dry your eyes before coming to God.

He is not afraid of your sorrow.

He meets you in it.

And He calls it sacred.

Devotional Insight

The Bible doesn't shy away from sorrow. It doesn't sanitize the emotions of its heroes. It invites us to see their tears—and by extension, our own—as holy offerings.

Jesus wept. Not once, but twice. First over the death of Lazarus, even knowing resurrection was moments away. Then again over Jerusalem, mourning a people who had missed the heart of God. The Savior of the world didn't withhold His tears. He allowed them to fall.

David, the mighty king and worshiper, filled the Psalms with his weeping. He cried out in fear, in grief, in loneliness. Yet God called him a man after His own heart—not in spite of his sorrow, but through it.

Jeremiah, the prophet whose ministry was marked by heartbreak, is remembered not only for his bold declarations but for his broken-hearted weeping. His tears were part of his calling.

Tears are part of the holy language of lament.
They are prayers without grammar.
Praise in its most vulnerable form.
Grief that refuses to be buried.

And they are not wasted.

God receives them. He writes them into your story. He holds them when you cannot. And in time, He transforms them—not always by removing the cause, but by redeeming the pain and drawing nearer than you ever imagined.

You don't have to hold it all together in God's presence. You just have to come.
With tears.
With silence.
With whatever you have left.

And there, in that sacred vulnerability, you will find that your weeping is not weakness. It is worship.

Guided Questions for Reflection

1. When was the last time I allowed myself to cry in God's presence?

2. What emotions am I holding back that God is inviting me to release?

3. How can I learn to see my tears as sacred rather than shameful?

Breath Prayer / Affirmation

My tears are safe with God.

Closing Prayer

God,
    You see my tears.
You hold every one.
    Thank You for welcoming me in my weeping.
    Help me stop hiding what hurts.
    Teach me that tears are a form of trust.
    In Jesus' name, Amen.

Your Reflections

Write what is real—your thoughts, your questions, your prayer.
Let honesty be your offering.

80

* * *

DEVOTION ELEVEN
When God Feels Far Away

Scripture Anchor:

"Truly, you are a God who hides himself,
O God of Israel, the Savior." — Isaiah 45:15

Opening Reflection

There are moments in the life of faith when everything goes still.

The prayers you once spoke with confidence now feel like whispers into the void.

The worship songs that once stirred your heart now fall flat.

The pages of Scripture feel quiet, and your spirit aches with questions no one seems to answer.

It's not that you've stopped believing.
It's that heaven feels… silent.

And in that silence, doubt creeps in.
Has God left me?
Did I miss something?
Why won't He speak?

But Scripture reminds us of a truth we often forget: silence is not absence.

God is not gone—He is hidden.

He is present in a different way.

A quieter way.

A deeper way.

Isaiah calls Him "a God who hides Himself." Not because He's playing games, but because there are dimensions of His presence only discovered in stillness. In waiting. In the hush between the notes.

It's in these moments that our roots grow.

Not in the spotlight of miracles, but in the soil of mystery.

Faith in the silence is not lesser faith.

It is seasoned faith. Refined faith.

Faith that walks by trust, not by sight.

So if God feels far, know this: He is closer than you think.

Even when He hides, He is still holding you.

Devotional Insight

The story of Scripture is not just one of voices and visions—it is also one of silence.

Job, after losing everything, sat in silence.

Scraping his wounds.

Waiting for God to speak. And for what must have felt like an eternity, heaven stayed quiet. No answers. No rescue. Just the long ache of not knowing. And yet, Job held on.

Mary and **Martha** waited four days for Jesus to arrive after their brother Lazarus died.

Each hour passed like a question:

Where is He?

Why hasn't He come?

They knew Jesus loved them. They had seen His power. But in that moment, He delayed. And in the silence, grief grew. And yet, they still called Him Lord when He arrived.

Jesus, on the cross, cried out, *"My God, my God, why have You forsaken Me?"* The Son of God Himself tasted silence so we could know we are never alone in it. Even in the absence of God's voice, Jesus trusted the heart of the Father.

Silence is not the end of the story. It is a chapter in the sacred journey. A season where God shifts from the God who *answers* to the God who *abides*.

In silence, He teaches us to lean not on our feelings but on His character. To trust the promises written long before the silence began. To believe that He is still working, still moving, even when we cannot see or hear Him.

You may not feel Him.

But you are still held.

Still loved.

Still seen.

And when the silence lifts—and it will—you'll find that something in you has changed.

You've grown.

You've rooted.

You've learned to trust in the dark.

And that is sacred.

Guided Questions for Reflection

1. What does silence from God feel like for me?

2. How can I stay rooted in truth when my emotions waver?

3. What promises can I hold on to in the quiet seasons?

Breath Prayer / Affirmation

God is near, even in the silence.

Closing Prayer

Lord,

When I can't hear You, help me to trust that You still hear me.

Anchor me in Your Word.

Steady me with Your presence.

Teach me to walk by faith, not by what I feel.

Amen.

Your Reflections

Write what is real—your thoughts, your questions, your prayer.
Let honesty be your offering.

(Space to Breathe)

* * *

DEVOTION TWELVE

When Praise Has Been Changed Forever

Scripture Anchor:

"Yet I am always with you;
you hold me by my right hand." — Psalm 73:23

Opening Reflection

By the time you reach the end of a long season of pain, something in you has changed.

Not everything has healed.

Not every question has been answered.

But you are not who you were when this journey began.

You've learned that faith doesn't always arrive with clarity.

That praise doesn't always come dressed in certainty or strength.

Somewhere between the breaking and the rebuilding, between the tears you couldn't stop and the silence you couldn't escape, your understanding of worship has shifted.

You don't sing the way you used to.

You don't pray the way you once did.

You don't reach for God with the same confidence or vocabulary.

And yet—you're still here.

It may not feel like victory. It may not even feel intentional. Some days, it may feel like survival more than faith. But what has endured matters. Because the faith that remains after suffering is not shallow or borrowed.

It is tested.

Tempered.

True.

This kind of praise doesn't rush to resolve the pain or wrap it in spiritual language. It doesn't pretend the wounds didn't cost you something. It acknowledges the loss—of innocence, of certainty, of the version of faith you once held—and still chooses to stay.

Sometimes praise doesn't return as a song.

Sometimes it returns as presence.

As the quiet decision to remain open to God, even when nothing is clear.

You may feel changed by what you've been through—and you are. But changed does not mean abandoned. Weakened does not mean forgotten. What remains in you is not the absence of faith, but the evidence of it.

You are still here.

And the God who has carried you this far has never let go.

Devotional Insight

The psalmist in Psalm 73 is not celebrating when he says, "Yet I am always with you."

He is confessing it.

He had wrestled with doubt.

He had nearly lost his footing.

He had questioned the goodness of God and the fairness of life.

And still—yet—he remained.

That word matters.

Yet.

Yet I am with You.

Yet You hold my hand.

This is not naïve faith.

This is faith that has been tested and tempered.

It is the faith that does not disappear when answers don't come.

The faith that does not vanish when the silence lingers.

The faith that remains—not because it is strong, but because God is.

You may feel changed by what you've been through. That doesn't mean you've been damaged beyond repair.

As a quiet trust that says, "I don't understand, but I'm still here."

And that kind of praise is not lesser.

It is deeper.

Guided Questions for Reflection

1. How has my faith changed through this season?

2. What parts of my old understanding have fallen away—and what has remained?

3. Where do I sense God still holding me, even now?

Breath Prayer / Affirmation

I am still here. I am still held.

Closing Prayer

God,
I don't worship the way I once did.
Some things have been lost along the way.
But You have not left me.
Thank You for holding me when I didn't know how to hold on.
Thank You for staying when my strength ran thin.
Receive what remains of my praise—not because it is perfect, but because it is real.
I am still here.
And I trust that You are too.
In Jesus' name, Amen.

Your Reflections

Write what is real—your thoughts, your questions, your prayer.
Let honesty be your offering.

(Space to Breathe)

* * *

FINAL REFLECTION:

Worship That Rises from the Ruins

The journey through brokenness is never linear. It ebbs and flows. Some days you feel steady; other days you wonder if faith is even still present. But this much is true: nothing you carried through these pages has been wasted.

Every hallelujah whispered through tears was heard.

Every moment you chose to stay mattered.

Every quiet act of trust shaped something deeper than you could see at the time.

You have walked through lament, through weariness, through silence and surrender. And here you are—not untouched, not unchanged, but still present.

Still open.

Still held.

As you pause here, take a moment to notice what has shifted—not what has been fixed, but what has been formed. Praise may not come easily or sound the way it once did, but it has grown roots. It has learned how to live alongside pain. It has learned how to stay.

This is the worship that rises from the ruins—not loud or polished, but steady. Honest. Sacred.

So keep walking.

Keep showing up.

Let your broken hallelujahs continue their quiet work.

They are building something holy.

* * *

CLOSING BLESSING:

You Are Not Alone

May you remember that even in the silence, God is still near.

May your pain become a place of encounter—not abandonment.

May your weakness remain a window to grace,
and your sorrow a seed of praise.

May you lift your hallelujahs—however broken—trusting they rise like incense.

May you rest in the truth that your worship matters, that your story is sacred, and that your journey is gently held by a God who redeems, restores, and renews.

You are not alone.
You are held.
You are loved.
Amen.

ACKNOWLEDGMENTS

To God, my strength and my song, who meets me in every shattered place and remains faithful when praise comes quietly and faith feels thin.

To my family and friends, whose love, prayers, and steady presence continually remind me that grace is not abstract—but lived and tangible. You have been light through many valleys.

To the readers, thank you for trusting me with your time, your stories, and your hearts. May these pages walk with you on hard days and gently remind you that even in the silence, you are seen and held.

READER'S GUIDE

REFLECTION PROMPTS

Whether you're walking through this devotional on your own, with a trusted companion, or within a small group, these prompts are offered as gentle invitations—not expectations. This is not a race to the final page. Let the journey unfold slowly. Let it remain sacred.

For Each Devotion:

As you reflect, consider sitting with one or two of these questions rather than all of them. Let what rises be enough.

- What part of this devotion feels closest to my own story right now?
- Was there a line or scripture that lingered after reading?
- How did this devotion expand—or gently challenge—my understanding of worship through brokenness?
- What truth from this section do I want to carry into the coming days?
- Is there an emotion, memory, or question I'm being invited to name more honestly?

There is no "right" pace. These practices are simply guides to help you remain present with God and with yourself.

- **Read Slowly:** Move through one devotion per week if possible. Let the words settle without rushing ahead.

- **Return Often**: Revisit the breath prayer throughout the week—especially in moments of fatigue, silence, or longing.

- **Write Freely:** Use the Your Reflections pages as space for truth-telling, not performance. Write what is real.

- **Sit with God:** After each devotion or prayer, pause for one or two minutes in silence. Let the quiet become part of your worship.

- **Gather Gently:** If reading with others, choose one reflection question and close your time with stillness or shared prayer.

You don't have to move quickly.
You don't have to have everything figured out.
This space is for you.
And God is already here.

WANT MORE ROOM TO HEAL?

If these devotions stirred something deep
and you find yourself longing for more space to process,
to grieve, to reflect, or to worship in your own way—

Shattered Praise: The Journal is a gentle companion to this devotional, created to support deeper healing, private worship, and honest reflection.

Within its pages, you'll find extended prompts, generous space to write, and quiet guidance for the parts of your praise still taking shape. There is no pressure to resolve everything at once. This is an invitation to continue the journey slowly, at your own pace.

You don't have to have all the answers.
You don't have to heal all at once.

There is still room.
There is still time.
There is sacred space for you.

Shattered Praise: The Journal is available wherever books are sold. To learn more, visit www.scribeandcanvas.com

If you're looking for printable tools, group resources, or a free companion packet, you can scan the QR code or visit:
www.scribeandcanvas.com/resources